IT'S A CHILD'S WORLD

*G*rowing Up Healthy

Using Nonfiction to Promote Literacy Across the Curriculum

by Doris Roettger

Fearon Teacher Aids
Simon & Schuster Supplementary Education Group

Teacher Reviewers

Judy Dierker
Roanoke, Virginia

Gwen Detlefsen
Manning, Iowa

Nora Forester
San Antonio, Texas

Connie Herman
Roanoke, Virginia

Delphine Hetes
Detroit, Michigan

Debbie Kellogg
West Des Moines, Iowa

Paulette Myers
Colo, Iowa

Sheila Valdez
Sacramento, California

Editorial Director: Virginia L. Murphy
Editor: Virginia Massey Bell
Copyeditor: Lisa Schwimmer
Illustration: Anita Nelson
Design: Terry McGrath
Cover Design: Lucyna Green

ISBN 0-86653-970-0

Printed in the United States of America
1.9 8 7 6 5 4 3 2 1

A Note from the Author

 $\mathcal{C}$ hildren have a natural curiosity about the world in which they live. They are intensely interested in learning about real things, real places, and real people. They also enjoy and learn from hands-on experiences. Nonfiction books and magazines provide opportunities for children to explore their many interests and extend their base of knowledge.

Reading nonfiction materials is different from reading picture or storybooks. To be effective readers, children need to learn how to locate information or find answers to their many questions. They also need to learn to think about and evaluate the accuracy of any information presented. Finally, they need opportunities to learn the relationship between what they read and the activities in which they apply their new knowledge.

You, as the teacher, can provide opportunities for children to learn from their observations, their reading, and their writing in an integrated language-arts approach across the curriculum.

Modeling thinking strategies and then providing practice across the curriculum will help students become observers and explorers of their world, plus effective users of literacy skills. Encouraging children to extend and demonstrate their understanding through a variety of communication areas—speaking, reading, drama, writing, listening, and art—is also very valuable.

The suggestions in this guide are action-oriented and designed to involve students in the thinking process. The activities do not relate to any one single book. Instead, the strategies and activities are designed to be used with any of the books suggested in the bibliography or with books found in your own media center. The suggested interdisciplinary activities can also be used across grade levels.

Each lesson begins with the reading of a nonfiction book, book chapter, or magazine article—any title that relates to the follow-up activities. During the activity phase and at other class times, students are encouraged to return to the nonfiction selections available in the classroom to find answers to their questions, compare and verify their observations, and add any new information to their current knowledge base.

The individual theme units are designed to be used for any length of time—from a few days to a month or more, depending on the needs and interests of your students.

Suggested goals for this unit are provided near the beginning of this guide on page 16. The webs on pages 7–9 give you an overview of the areas in which activities are provided.

On each page of this guide, there is space for you to write reflective notes as well as ideas that you want to remember for future teaching. This guide is designed to be a resource from which you make decisions and then select the learning experiences that will be most appropriate for your students.

Doris Roettger

Contents

Literacy Skills

The following literacy skills are addressed in the *Growing Up Healthy* theme guide.

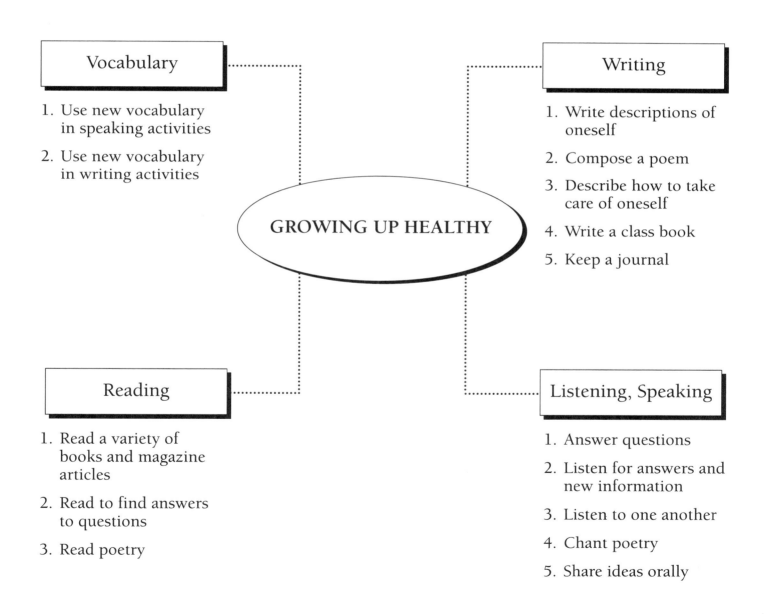

Vocabulary

1. Use new vocabulary in speaking activities
2. Use new vocabulary in writing activities

Writing

1. Write descriptions of oneself
2. Compose a poem
3. Describe how to take care of oneself
4. Write a class book
5. Keep a journal

GROWING UP HEALTHY

Reading

1. Read a variety of books and magazine articles
2. Read to find answers to questions
3. Read poetry

Listening, Speaking

1. Answer questions
2. Listen for answers and new information
3. Listen to one another
4. Chant poetry
5. Share ideas orally

Interdisciplinary Skills

$\mathcal{T}$he following interdisciplinary skills are addressed in the *Growing Up Healthy* theme guide.

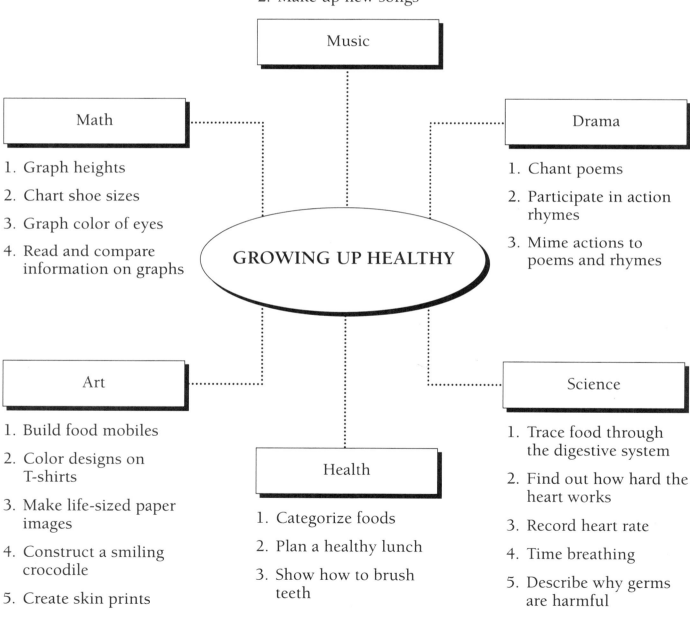

1. Learn and sing songs
2. Make up new songs

Music

Math

1. Graph heights
2. Chart shoe sizes
3. Graph color of eyes
4. Read and compare information on graphs

GROWING UP HEALTHY

Drama

1. Chant poems
2. Participate in action rhymes
3. Mime actions to poems and rhymes

Art

1. Build food mobiles
2. Color designs on T-shirts
3. Make life-sized paper images
4. Construct a smiling crocodile
5. Create skin prints

Health

1. Categorize foods
2. Plan a healthy lunch
3. Show how to brush teeth

Science

1. Trace food through the digestive system
2. Find out how hard the heart works
3. Record heart rate
4. Time breathing
5. Describe why germs are harmful

Learning and Working Strategies

The following learning and working strategies are addressed in the *Growing Up Healthy* theme guide.

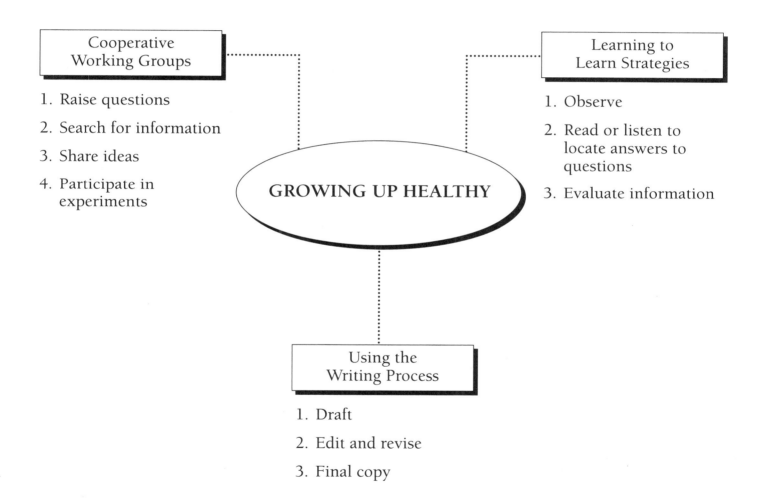

Cooperative Working Groups

1. Raise questions
2. Search for information
3. Share ideas
4. Participate in experiments

GROWING UP HEALTHY

Learning to Learn Strategies

1. Observe
2. Read or listen to locate answers to questions
3. Evaluate information

Using the Writing Process

1. Draft
2. Edit and revise
3. Final copy

About Growing Up Healthy

$\mathcal{G}$ood nutrition and health are vital to a happy life, and learning about good health at an early age gives children an important head start toward healthy living. In this unit, children learn the value of keeping themselves healthy, as well as learning how they grow, how their bodies work, and why exercise is important.

Many changes have occurred in the last few years in regard to nutrition. The U.S. Department of Agriculture and nutritionists now widely recommend six rather than four food groups, with fruits, vegetables, and grains topping the list for good nutrition.

The term "You are what you eat" is actually quite true. What goes into the body determines how well our bodies work. Our bodies are made up of millions of cells and these cells need certain nutrients to keep our bodies healthy. The foods we choose to eat go to all parts of our bodies to replace worn out cells, as well as provide energy to keep all of our body parts working. Nutrients are the elements of food that are used to help us grow, keep our bodies working properly, and help our bodies repair itself.

Exercise is also essential to good health. Our bodies are like machines and need exercise in order to work properly. If our muscles don't get enough exercise, they become weak and are less able to help our bodies work efficiently. By staying in shape through exercise, we prepare our bodies for running, lifting, carrying, and so on. If we stay physically fit, we have more energy, look better, think more clearly, and feel better in our daily lives.

There are many organizations and publications with additional information for you and your students. Addresses and telephone numbers are available in your library or local directory. A few addresses are listed here for your convenience.

Child Life Magazine
Children's Better Health Institute
P.O. Box 1003
Des Moines, IA 50340

Current Health I
Field Publications
4343 Equity Drive
P.O. Box 16630
Columbus, OH 43216
1-800-999-7100

Monkeyshines
Health and Science
P.O. Box 10245
Greensboro, NC 27404

United States Department of Agriculture
14th St. and Independence Ave., SW
Washington, DC 20250
202-447-2798

Suggested Reading Selections

A variety of nonfiction and fiction selections for the primary grades is suggested for use with this theme unit. You will probably want to assemble a collection of materials ahead of time. Or, you may wish to have the students help collect several titles from the library as a group activity. The number and type of selections you and the children read will depend on the length of time you devote to this unit, as well as the availability of titles and the level of your students.

Nonfiction Books

Breathing by John Gaskin. New York: Franklin Watts, Inc., 1984. A nicely illustrated book explaining about lungs and how we breathe. Includes glossary and index.

Dinosaurs Alive and Well by Laurie Krasny Brown and Marc Brown. Boston: Little, Brown and Company, 1990. Information on nutrition, relationships with family and friends, exercise, and dealing with stress. Wonderful illustrations by Marc Brown.

Ears Are for Hearing by Paul Showers. New York: Thomas Y. Crowell, 1990. Describes how sound waves travel through the ear and leave signals for the brain to interpret.

Eating by John Gaskin. New York: Franklin Watts, Inc., 1984. In simple language with color illustrations, this book describes the different types of foods, why we need food, and what happens when we eat. A few projects and glossary included.

Every Kid's Guide to Nutrition and Health Care by Joy Berry. Chicago: Childrens Press, 1987. Explains proper nutrition and health care, including exercises, cleanliness, rest, sleep, and the need for fresh air.

The Eye and Seeing by Steve Parker. New York: Franklin Watts, Inc., 1989. Talks about the eyes and seeing. Illustrated.

Germs Make Me Sick! by Melvin Berger. New York: Thomas Y. Crowell, 1985. Child-oriented picture book describes how bacteria, germs, and viruses affect our bodies and how our bodies fight them. Colorful, fun illustrations by Marylin Hafner.

Health and Hygiene by Brian R. Ward. New York: Franklin Watts, Inc., 1988. Photographs and illustrations. Explains why hygiene is important to health as well as describing diseases and infections.

The Healthy Habits Handbook by Slim Goodbody. New York: Coward-McCann, Inc., 1983. An entertaining book that demonstrates and explains healthy habits. Helps children understand their role in keeping themselves healthy. Illustrations.

The Human Body: The Digestive System by Kathleen Elgin. New York: Franklin Watts, Inc., 1973. Simple illustrations with informative text. Describes the function of each part of the digestive system.

The Human Body: The Heart by Kathleen Elgin. New York: Franklin Watts, Inc., 1968. Simply written text geared towards the child explains how the heart works.

Junk Food—What It Is, What It Does by Judith S. Seixas. New York: Greenwillow Books, 1984. A simply stated introduction to junk food, what is in each food, and how each food affects the body.

The Magic School Bus: Inside the Body by Joanna Cole. New York: Scholastic Inc., 1988. The magic bus takes children on a special trip to get a close-up view of the major parts of the body and see how each works. Vivid, colorful illustrations.

The Mystery of Sleep by Alvin and Virginia Silverstein. Boston: Little, Brown and Company, 1987. Some illustrations. Discusses why we need sleep, dreams, animal sleeping, and sleeping problems.

Nutrition by Leslie Jean LeMaster. Chicago: Childrens Press, 1985. Explains what our bodies need and discusses vitamins, proteins, carbohydrates, and water.

The Story of Your Ear by Alvin and Virginia Silverstein. New York: Coward-McCann, Inc., 1981. Talks about the structure and functions of the ear, how sound travels, selective hearing, noise pollution, and balance.

Talkabout Growing by Henry Pluckrose. New York: Franklin Watts, Inc., 1988. Very simple book with photos about growing.

Thinkabout Hearing by Henry Pluckrose. New York: Franklin Watts, Inc., 1986. Very simple book with photos about hearing.

What Happens to a Hamburger? by Paul Showers. New York: Thomas Y. Crowell, 1985. Brightly illustrated book details what happens when we eat a hamburger and other foods. Child-oriented.

Your Heart and Blood by Leslie Jean LeMaster. Chicago: Childrens Press, 1984. Discusses the importance of blood to the body and the role the heart plays. Simple text.

Your Heart and Lungs by Dorothy Baldwin and Claire Lister. New York: Bookwright Press, 1984. Explains in detail how the heart and lungs work as well as how to take care of them.

Fiction Books

Albert the Running Bear's Exercise Book by Barbara Isenberg and Marjorie Jaffe. New York: Clarion Books, 1984. Albert shows children exercises to help keep them healthy. Lively illustrations and story.

Babies by Rachel Isadora. New York: Greenwillow Books, 1990. Babies enjoy daily activities, such as eating, dressing, bathing, and sleeping.

Blueberries for Sal by Robert McCloskey. New York: Puffin, 1976. A wonderful story about a little girl and a bear cub who both wander away from their mothers while picking blueberries.

Cherries and Cherry Pits by Vera B. Williams. New York: Greenwillow Books, 1986. Bidemi draws pictures and tells stories about cherries.

Cloudy with a Chance of Meatballs by Judith Barrett. New York: Atheneum, 1978. Food drops from the sky and delights young readers!

Eat Your Peas, Louise! by Pegeen Snow. Chicago: Childrens Press, 1985. A picture book story in rhyme.

Gregory, the Terrible Eater by Mitchell Sharmat. New York: Macmillan, 1980. An illustrated storybook about a little goat named Gregory who likes to eat fruits and vegetables rather than clothing, paper, and shoes.

The Growing Story by Ruth Krauss. New York: Harper & Row, 1947. A picture book about how all living things grow. Full-page illustrations.

Here Are My Hands by Bill Martin, Jr., and John Archambault. New York: Henry Holt and Company, 1987. Well-illustrated book showing what we can do with our hands.

I Need a Lunchbox by Jeanette Caines. New York: Harper & Row, 1988. A little boy dreams of owning a lunchbox, even before he has started school.

My Feet by Aliki. New York: Thomas Y. Crowell, 1990. Brightly illustrated book describes the foot and what the foot helps us do.

My Hands by Aliki. New York: Thomas Y. Crowell, 1990. Describes the hand and what our hands help us do. Nicely illustrated.

Sleep Is for Everyone by Paul Showers. New York: Thomas Y. Crowell, 1974. A picture storybook teaches children the need for sleep and what happens when we sleep well.

Stone Soup by Ann McGovern. New York: Scholastic, Inc., 1986. A hungry young man, who is refused a meal by an old woman, makes soup from a stone.

Stone Soup: An Old Tale by Marcia Brown. New York: Scribner's, 1975. The story of three hungry soldiers who are able to conjure up a feast by making soup from three stones.

This Is the Bread I Baked for Ned by Crescent Dragonwagon. New York: Macmillan, 1989. Glenda prepares a wonderful meal for Ned which is quickly eaten by several hungry guests. Written in verse.

Teacher Reference

Be a Frog, a Bird, or a Tree by Rachel Carr. Garden City, New York: Doubleday & Company, 1973. Yoga exercises for children in verse. Movements are illustrated in photography.

Blood and Guts: A Working Guide to Your Own Insides by Linda Allison and David Katz. Boston: Little, Brown and Company, 1976. A thorough book that discusses the many elements of the human body and how it works. Includes activities and experiments.

Bodyworks: The Kids' Guide to Food and Physical Fitness by Carol Bershad and Deborah Bernick. New York: Random House, 1979. Well-written, child-oriented guide discusses how the body works. Includes large sections on nutrition, exercise, and food, as well as the heart and lungs. Contains a lot of information.

Now We Are Six by A. A. Milne. New York: E. P. Dutton, 1927. Poems and verse by the author of *Winnie the Pooh*.

Stamp Your Feet by Sarah Hays and Toni Goffe. New York: Lothrop, Lee and Shepard Books, 1988. Traditional rhymes with illustrations of body movements.

Instructional Goals

$\mathcal{I}$nstructional goals for this theme unit are provided here. Space is also provided so that you may fill in your own individual goals where appropriate as well. By the end of this theme unit, students should be able to:

1. Describe how they are like other people.
2. Describe who they were as babies and toddlers.
3. Raise questions about growing up based on their own curiosity.
4. Find information to answer their questions.
5. Perform experiments, observe results, and share information with classmates.
6. Create mobiles to demonstrate their understanding of healthy foods.
7. Trace food through the digestive system.
8. Perform a variety of exercises.
9. Share with others what they have learned about their eyes, ears, and teeth.
10. Use new vocabulary in their speaking and writing.
11. Write about what they have learned.
12. Share what they have learned through drama, art, and writing.
13. ....
14. ....
15. ....
16. ....
17. ....
18. ....
19. ....
20. ....

Getting Started

What Do We Already Know?

*T*he following activities are designed to help launch the *Growing Up Healthy* theme unit. You may want to use all of the activities or only one or two, depending on the needs of your students. At the beginning of each lesson, reading a nonfiction book or magazine selection to the class serves as a motivator and helps students become more familiar with and involved in using nonfiction selections. For the activities in this section, a general selection on health and nutrition would probably be most appropriate. You'll also want to provide plenty of opportunities for children to return to nonfiction selections independently during the activity phases and at other times during class periods as well.

1. Finding Out What Children Already Know

Find out what the children already know about growth and what their misperceptions and questions are so that you can help direct their learning.

a. Ask children to name what they think they know about growing up and staying healthy. Write their suggestions on a large sheet of paper.

b. List what the children think they know about growing up and staying healthy, but are not certain about, in a second column.

c. Ask children to raise questions they have about growing up and staying healthy and list the questions in a third column. Leave enough space so that you can record possible sources to check for information.

d. As a class, decide which questions the group would like to answer.

e. Keep this chart posted in the classroom and use it to continue discussion and relate the information to other areas throughout the unit.

Facts We Know About Growing Up Healthy	What We Think We Know	Questions We Have and Things We Wonder About	What We Have Learned

2. Introducing the Books

a. Introduce children to the books they will be using as they study about health and growing up. Share each book by reading the title aloud and then paging through the book so children can see the book's content. Explain the types of information they will find in each book.

b. Display all the books in the classroom reading center. Encourage children to visit the center often.

3. Vocabulary

List the following vocabulary words on chart paper and then display the chart in the classroom. Display pictures representing growth and health, such as exercises, sports, food charts, and so on. As you use the vocabulary words during discussions about growth and staying healthy, point out the vocabulary words on the chart.

foot	heartbeat
hand	muscle
height	breathe
eyes	lungs
ears	esophagus
teeth	stomach
fingernails	small intestines
sleep	digestion
exercise	high-energy foods

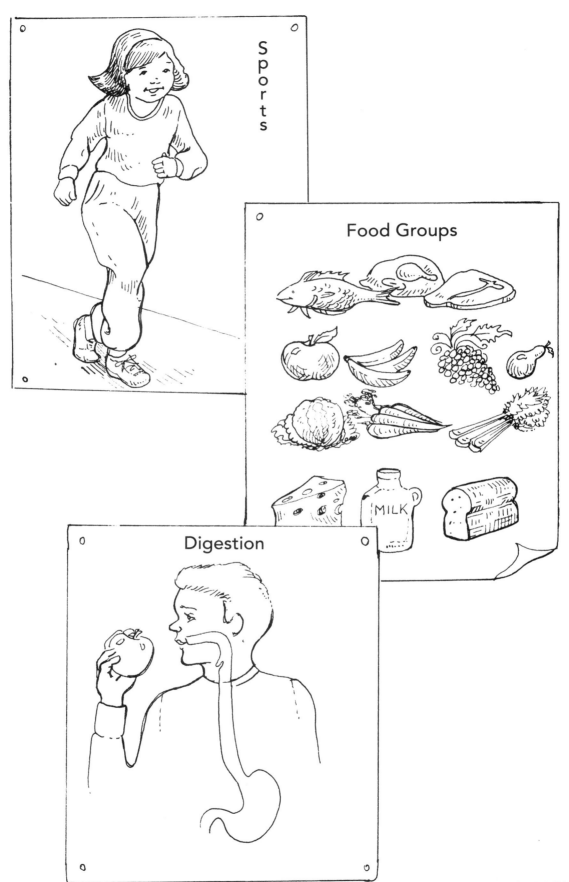

Sports

Food Groups

MILK

Digestion

When We Were Younger

*C*hildren delight in knowing what they were like when they were babies and how they have changed over the years. The activities in this section help children learn how different they are now from the way they were as babies and toddlers. A letter asking parents to send to school a baby picture, an article of baby or toddler clothing, an article of clothing from a year ago that is now too small, a toy, and a T-shirt (for later activities) is provided on page 58.

1. Baby Pictures

a. Pique children's curiosity by wondering aloud what they were like when they were babies. Encourage the children to raise similar questions. Then ask children how they might find the answers to their many questions.

b. Ask parents to send one or two snapshots of their child as a baby (see the reproducible letter on page 58). Use yarn to create a timeline showing the months and the years in which the children were born. Cluster the baby pictures according to the appropriate months.

2. Display of Children's Clothing and Toys

a. Ask parents to send in an item of baby or toddler clothing that their child wore when he or she was an infant. Also, ask children if they can bring in a toy they used to play with when they were younger. A reproducible letter is provided for your convenience on page 58.

b. Create a display of clothes and toys for babies and toddlers so that children can see what they wore then and the types of toys they used to play with. Remind the children that these items are borrowed and discuss the importance of handling the toys and clothing carefully. Note: Some children will not have items that they can bring to school. Encourage these children to bring a baby brother's or sister's clothing or toy—or even a neighbor's.

3. Unbirthday Party

Plan an Unbirthday Party. Invite the children to sing the "Unbirthday Song" from Walt Disney's *Alice in Wonderland*. Chart each child's birthday on a calendar and display the calendar in the classroom. Bring special treats for the party and celebrate all the growing that we do throughout the year.

Who We Are Now

*I*n this section, children will be recording their height, the size of their hands and feet, and the color of their eyes. These activities help children document specific information about themselves. Before beginning the activities in this section, share one or more nonfiction selections relating to the lesson.

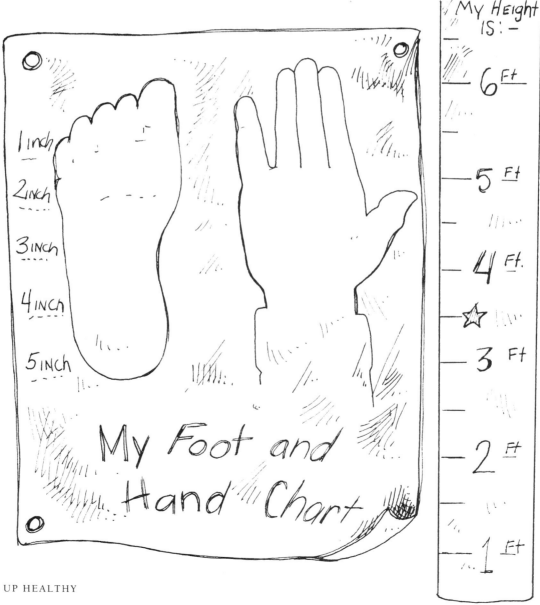

1. The Way We Look

Using a Polaroid camera, take a snapshot of each child. Have the children write or dictate their names and the date of the photograph on the back of the picture with a marker. Display the pictures on a bulletin board entitled "Who We Are and How We Look."

a. Ask the children if they can guess how many inches tall they are. Then measure and record the height, in inches, of each child. You'll want to include yourself, too.

b. Have each child cut a strip of adding-machine tape the same length as his or her height. For easy identification, color code each of the lengths, such as yellow for 42 inches, orange for 43 inches, and so on. Have the children write or dictate their names and the date on their strips.

c. Create a life-size bar graph next to the bulletin board by displaying the strips in increasing order of height.

d. Ask the children to decide how many children are the same height and how many inches difference there is between the tallest and the shortest child.

2. How Large Are Our Feet and Hands?

a. Ask the children if they can guess how big their feet are in inches. Record the children's guesses on the chalkboard. Have the children take off their socks and shoes. Encourage the children to compare the size of their feet with the other students in the class.

b. Spread newspaper on the floor. Place large pans of different-colored tempera paint on the newspaper. Have available pans of warm, soapy water as well. Give each child a sheet of construction paper. One at a time, ask the children to carefully step in the color of paint of their choice and then carefully step onto the sheet of construction paper to make footprints. Ask each child to step into a pan of warm, soapy water after making his or her prints to rinse off the feet. Have the children write or dictate their names and the date on their footprints. Encourage the children to compare their footprints with their estimated foot sizes. Display the footprints on a wall ranging from the smallest to the largest.

c. Have children trace around their right or left hand on construction paper and then cut out the handprint. Younger children may trace each other's hands. Ask children to write or dictate their names and the date on their handprints. Have the children compare their handprints. Which hands are the smallest? Which are the largest? Glue each child's handprints on a sheet of butcher paper. Encourage the children to color in a head and body for a "Me" poster. Display the "Me" posters in the classroom.

3. What Color Are Our Eyes?

a. Cut blue, brown, black, and green 2-inch squares from construction paper. Ask whether anyone in the class has a different eye color, such as hazel or gray, and cut squares of paper in that color, too. Start a color bar graph.

b. Ask each child the color of his or her eyes. Give each child a matching-colored square and encourage the children to glue their squares in the appropriate place on the color bar graph. Have the children stack the squares one above the other to make the bar graph.

Real-Life Laboratory

Eyes, Ears, and Teeth

Children learn about their eyes, ears, and teeth and how to take care of them through the activities in this section. Begin each lesson by reading a nonfiction selection relating to the activity or activities. You may also want to include some fiction selections as well.

1. Our Eyes Are Important

Before beginning this activity, read *Arthur's Eyes* by Marc Brown aloud to the children. Invite a professional to school to talk with the children about eyes and their proper care. Ask the specialist to give the children a vision test. Have the specialist explain to the class why people wear glasses.

2. Our Ears Are Important

Read an appropriate nonfiction selection to the children before beginning this activity. Some books are suggested here:

> *Thinkabout Hearing* by Henry Pluckrose
>
> *Ears Are for Hearing* by Paul Showers
>
> *The Story of Your Ear* by Alvin and Virginia Silverstein

a. Show the children a diagram or model of an ear and explain how hearing works. If possible, ask a professional nurse or audiologist to come to school to speak to the class.

b. Divide the class into student pairs. Ask the nurse or audiologist to show each child, one at a time, how to look in their partner's ear using a pen flashlight or an audiologist's instrument.

c. Then ask children to very gently pull the lobe upwards to straighten the ear canal and look into their partner's ear again. What do they see?

3. Baby Teeth and Permanent Teeth

a. Find out how many children have lost some of their baby teeth. Chart the number of teeth all of the children as a group have lost. Add to the chart as children lose teeth throughout the year. Ask the children why they think they lose their baby teeth.

b. Explain to the children that they will eventually get 32 permanent teeth. Discuss what would happen if they would lose a permanent tooth.

4. Taking Care of Teeth

This is an activity that teaches children how to take good care of their teeth. Before beginning this activity, read aloud an appropriate nonfiction selection.

a. Invite a dental assistant to school to explain to the children why they need to brush and floss their teeth. Ask the dental assistant to demonstrate proper brushing and flossing techniques as well. Before the demonstration, ask the dental assistant about providing free toothpaste and toothbrushes for each child.

b. Divide the class into small cooperative working groups and ask the children to demonstrate how to brush and floss one's teeth. Then discuss why brushing and flossing are important for healthy teeth.

c. Suggest to the children that they keep a record of how often they brush their teeth for one week. Give each child a copy of the tooth calendar found on page 60 and a note to the parents (see page 59). At the end of the week, have the children bring their calendars back to share with the class.

d. Ask the students to suggest foods that they think might be bad for their teeth. Make a list on butcher paper. Then ask the children to suggest foods that they think might be good for their teeth. Make a separate list. Discuss these lists with the class.

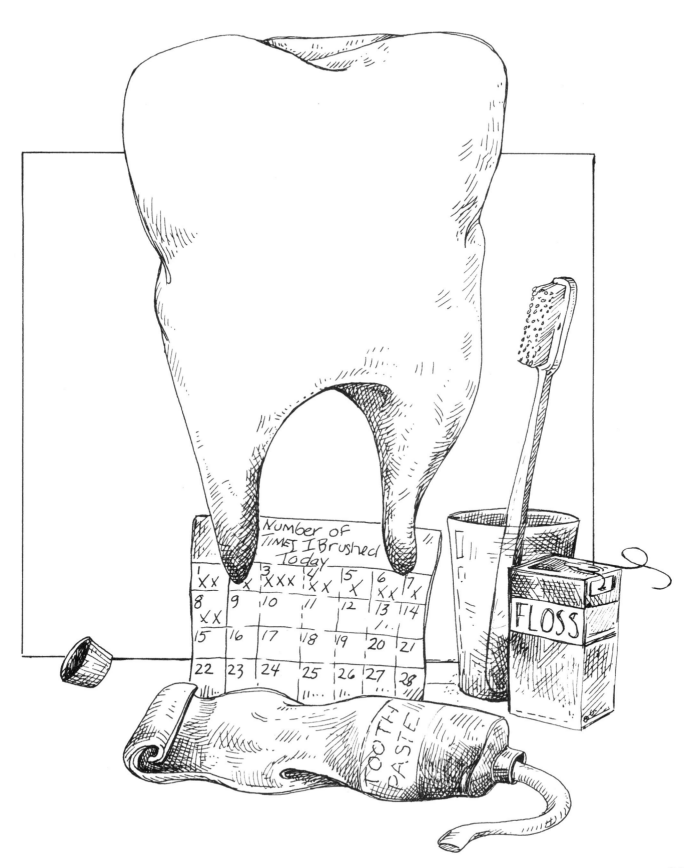

Number of
TIMES I Brushed
Today

1 XX		3 X	4 XXX	5 XX	6 X	7 X
8 XX	9	10	11	12	13	14
15	16	17	18	19	20	21
22	23	24	25	26	27	28

FLOSS

TOOTH PASTE

Food and Growing

$\mathcal{T}$he activities in this section are designed to help children become aware of those foods that are healthy and those that are not. In addition to reading a nonfiction selection on the relationship of food to growth, there are several wonderful fiction books on this topic that you may want to share with your students as well.

1. Raising Questions

a. Help children raise "I wonder" questions about what role food plays in our growth. For example,

"I wonder how food helps us grow."

"I wonder if some foods are better for us than others."

b. Encourage children to wonder aloud. Then list their questions on a large chart. Display the chart in the classroom so children can reread their questions. Or, place a tape recorder in a listening center. With the help of an older student, ask the children to record their questions, one at a time, on the tape recorder. Make the tape recorder available in the listening center so children can listen to their questions.

2. Food for Our Bodies

a. Read aloud to the students some selections from a number of books suggested in the bibliography. Then encourage discussion on why food is important to growth. To help children learn about food and growth, pose several questions. For example,

"How do we feel when we don't get enough food?"

"How well can we think when we're hungry?"

"I wonder why we get tired when we haven't eaten properly."

b. Record the children's responses in a web format. For beginning readers, use rebus writing or pictures when possible.

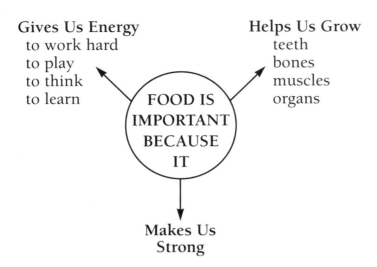

Gives Us Energy
to work hard
to play
to think
to learn

Helps Us Grow
teeth
bones
muscles
organs

FOOD IS IMPORTANT BECAUSE IT

Makes Us Strong

c. Create a second web about the four basic food groups. Ask children to give examples of each of the food groups and discuss how much they need to eat daily from each group in order to stay healthy. Provide examples as necessary.

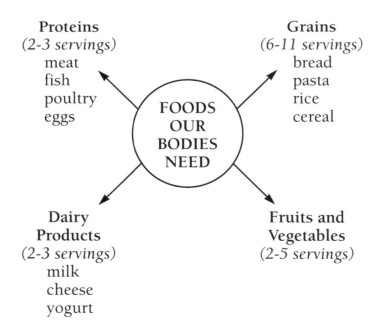

Proteins
(2-3 servings)
meat
fish
poultry
eggs

Grains
(6-11 servings)
bread
pasta
rice
cereal

FOODS OUR BODIES NEED

Dairy Products
(2-3 servings)
milk
cheese
yogurt

Fruits and Vegetables
(2-5 servings)

3. Fishing for Good Foods

NOTES

a. Provide old magazines so children can cut out pictures of foods from the four basic food groups. Encourage children to glue the pictures onto fish shapes. A fish pattern is provided on page 61. Slip a paper clip onto the front of each fish and put all the fish into a large bucket. For a fishing pole, tie a string onto a stick and tie a magnet onto the end of the string. Label four smaller buckets with the name of each food group.

b. Invite children to try to "catch" a fish by using the magnet to pick up the paper clip on the fish shapes. When students catch a fish, encourage them to think about and decide which group the food belongs to and then put the fish into the correct bucket.

4. Food Group Collage

Make a collage of each of the four basic food groups using pictures from magazines or packages from various food products.

5. Planning a School Lunch Menu

a. Invite a school cook to help plan one of the school's lunch menus with your class. Have the children write invitations to a parent or grandparent to join them for lunch the day the menu is served.

b. As an alternative to this activity, plan a special lunch as a class. Ask children to help make a menu that includes items from each of the four basic food groups. Ask guests to participate by contributing one of the items on the menu.

6. Foods We Ate As Babies

This activity helps children understand how their food needs change as they grow older.

a. Bring in samples of baby foods, such as baby food in jars, cereal, and formula. Ask the children to taste each of the foods.

b. Encourage discussion with questions. Discuss the differences and similarities between baby food and the types of foods the children eat today.

   1. What are the differences in the foods you ate when you were younger and the foods you eat now?

   2. Why is baby food different than the food you eat now?

   3. Why are you able to eat different foods now?

   4. Which tastes better, the baby food or the food you eat now?

7. Tracing Food Through Our Bodies

a. Conduct a class experiment to learn how our digestive system works. Give each child a cracker to eat. Ask the children to touch their throats as they swallow and describe how it feels. Ask the question "Where does the food go next?"

b. Make a transparency of the digestive system using an illustration from an encyclopedia. Read an appropriate book about the digestive system, such as *The Magic School Bus: Inside the Body* by Joanne Cole. Have the children identify the following:

esophagus	the long tube from our throat to our stomach
stomach	a sack-like organ between the ribs, just above the waist, where the food goes when it leaves the esophagus
small intestine	a long curled-up tube under the stomach that takes the valuable parts of the food that our bodies need into the bloodstream
large intestine	a larger curled-up tube just below the waist where all the unused food parts go

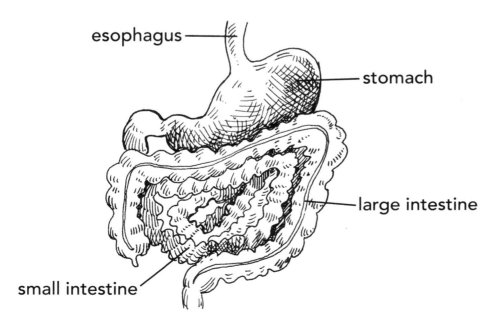

esophagus — stomach

large intestine

small intestine

Exercise, Growing, and Staying Healthy

*G*ood healthy habits involve many things—such as exercise, getting enough sleep, keeping clean, and not spreading germs. Exercise provides opportunities for children to develop body strength and flexibility. Select one or two books or articles relating to the activity or activities to share with students before beginning each lesson.

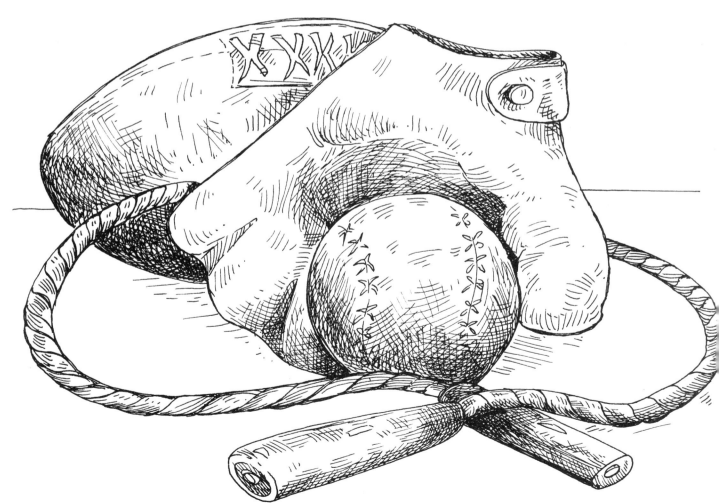

1. How Babies Exercise

Invite children who have baby brothers and sisters to describe how a baby gets exercise. Ask students to show the rest of the class what their baby brothers and sisters do. Discuss the differences in what children of different ages can do for exercise and why.

2. Exercise Club

a. Read appropriate fiction and nonfiction selections to the children before beginning the activities. Some suggestions are:

> *The Human Body: The Heart* by Kathleen Elgin
>
> *Your Heart and Blood* by Leslie Jean LeMaster
>
> *Bodyworks: The Kids' Guide to Food and Physical Fitness* by Carol Bershad and Deborah Bernick
>
> *Albert the Running Bear's Exercise Book* by Barbara Isenberg and Marjorie Jaffe

b. Organize an exercise club. As a group, decide what children need to know to join the club and when, where, and how often the club will meet. You might want to work with the physical education teacher on this activity. Make up membership cards (see page 62 for patterns). Then discuss the value of exercise on the muscles and the heart. Teach the children to take their pulse. Show the children how to place two fingers on their wrists. Ask what they feel. Explain the relationship between pulse and heartbeat. Have the children take their pulse once a week before and after each of their exercises. On a chart, list the exercises and the heart rates for each child. Have the children compare how the different exercises affect their heart rate.

c. Do safe exercises with your students. Show the children each exercise before asking them to try it themselves. Watch carefully as the students perform each exercise to make sure they are exercising in a safe and correct manner.

Stretching

Lie on your back with your arms and legs flat on the floor. Stretch your arms above your head. Stretch your legs as far as they will go.

Chopping

Chop wood by standing with your feet apart and clasping your hands over your head. Bend back as far as you can comfortably go, then bend forward and down. Let your arms swing between your legs. Repeat ten times.

Crunches

Lie on your back with your arms crossed on your chest and your knees bent. Slowly lift your head and roll your shoulders toward your knees. Try to lift your shoulders off the ground. Then return to the starting position. Remember to keep your knees bent. See how many crunches you can do in one minute.

Arm Circles

Stand with your legs shoulder-width apart. Stretch your arms out to the sides with the palms of your hands up. Make large circles with your arms. Move the arms forward and then back. Repeat five times. Drop your arms, wiggle them, and relax. Gradually work up to ten circles. Repeat the exercise, with the palms of your hands facing down.

Push-Ups

Lean forward on your hands and knees. Bend your arms, lean forward, and touch your nose to the floor. Try not to let your stomach touch the floor. Push yourself up by straightening your arms. Do as many push-ups as you can without straining yourself.

Skip-Walk-Run-Walk

Go around the gym or track four times. For the first lap, skip around the track. For the second, walk fast. On the third lap, run as fast as you can. Then on the last lap, walk fast again.

d. After exercising, play soft music to relax and cool down. Walk around the track or room, moving slowly with the music. Then have the children take their pulses once again.

e. Set aside time to discuss with the students how exercise affects them. Ask questions to stimulate discussion. For example,

> Can you do more exercises now than you could when you started?
>
> Do you feel better physically?
>
> Why do you think exercise is good for you?

3. Field Day

Have a field day at the end of the unit. Plan lots of active games for individuals, partners, and teams. Invite parents, grandparents, or another class to join in the festivities.

4. Recording Sleep Time

Ask the children to draw the hands on a face of a clock that show when they go to bed at night and when they get up. Students who are able to tell time can write the notation as well. As a group, discuss the amount of sleep children usually need each night.

5. Keeping Clean

a. Read appropriate books or sections of books pertaining to the importance of keeping our bodies clean. Some suggested books are *Germs Make Me Sick!* by Melvin Berger and *The Healthy Habits Handbook* by Slim Goodbody. Discuss how germs can make us sick and the benefits of keeping clean, washing hands, bathing, and so on.

b. Encourage the children to wash their hands with soap and water when they return from recess and before they eat lunch. Point out the importance of washing hands after using the bathroom as well.

6. Colds and Coughs

a. Ask the children how many of them have ever had a cold or cough. Invite children to describe how they felt.

b. Encourage children to speculate on how they might have gotten their colds and what they could do to avoid getting sick. Ask children to find books in the reading center that might have information on how to avoid colds. Share the books with the class.

c. To help children see how germs are spread when they cough and sneeze, ask them to hold their hands in front of the mouths and pretend to sneeze. Explain that all the moisture they feel is filled with germs when they are sick.

d. As a group, decide what people should do when they cough or sneeze. List the children's ideas on a chart. Encourage children to draw illustrations that show what to do and what not to do if they have a cold.

Cross-Curriculum Activities

Writing Arena

*W*riting helps children think about what they have observed and what they already know. It also helps them synthesize their thoughts and then communicate their ideas to others. Read a nonfiction selection to the class before beginning a writing activity. You might point out some sentences or paragraphs in the selection that are especially well-written.

1. Describing Growth

a. Ask children to bring in an article of clothing, such as a shirt or jacket that they wore last year that is now too small for them (see the reproducible letter on page 58). Take pictures of the students wearing the clothing. Encourage the children to discuss how much they have grown in the last year and how they feel in their clothes that are now too small.

b. Help the children write a few sentences describing how they feel about growing bigger and how big they would like to get someday. Encourage children to share with the class or a partner what they have written. Create a bulletin-board display of the pictures and writings.

2. Writing a Description

a. Read aloud to the class the poem "The End" by A. A. Milne.

b. Share with the children something you did when you were very young. Then encourage the children to share things they can remember or that family members have told them that they did or said when they were younger. For a homework assignment, ask the children to interview a family member or members. Ask the family members to recall some events from the past. Encourage the students to share the interviews with their classmates.

c. Send home the fill-in-the-blank worksheet entitled "About Me" provided on page 63. Ask parents to help their child complete the worksheet and then return it to school.

d. Provide opportunities for children to read the description of themselves on the worksheet to the class.

3. Writing Poems

a. Invite the children to recall healthy foods they have learned about during this unit. Encourage them to think of other healthy foods, too. List all the foods on a large sheet of paper by categories.

b. As a class, write a poem about healthy foods. Display the finished poems in the classroom at the children's eye level.

4. Newsletter to Parents

Hold a class meeting to have children look over all the writings, pictures, and other projects they have created during the *Growing Up Healthy* theme unit. Suggest that students write a newsletter to their parents about the unit. Compile all the pictures and writings in a newsletter format. Provide space for parents' comments. Send home a copy for each parent.

5. I Take Good Care of Myself

a. Ask the children to recall ways that they can take care of themselves—their teeth, their eyes and ears, exercise, what kinds of foods they eat, and how much sleep they get. Then have children draw a picture of themselves taking good care of themselves.

b. Have children share their drawings in small cooperative working groups. Display the pictures on a bulletin board. Later, encourage the children to include these pictures in a story about themselves.

6. Class Book on Growing Up Healthy

a. Suggest to the children that the class write a big book about growing up healthy. Discuss what they want to include in the book. List the items on the board or on a large sheet of paper.

b. Encourage children to tell what information they have learned about each of the items listed. Write the information on a large chart tablet. Leave a space between each line for any needed changes. This writing may take several days.

c. Have the class reread the draft of their big book. As they are reading, ask the children whether the information makes sense and sounds right. Write the changes in the space between the lines. As a group, decide the sentences that should go on each page of the final book.

d. Copy the information into final form. Leave space for the illustrations. List all the children's names on the title page. Read the book together frequently. Then arrange for the children to visit other classes to read the book aloud. If possible, display the book in the library, too.

Art All Around

Art activities help children visualize the concepts they have been reading about and discussing. Frequently, through art, children will want to review something they have read, heard, or observed so that their artwork is as accurate as they can make it. You'll want to have several resources available for children to refer to. Select a book or magazine article with good photographs or illustrations to read aloud to the class before beginning any activity or activities.

1. Food Mobiles

a. Divide the class into four cooperative working groups. Assign each group to one of the following: breakfast, lunch, dinner, or snacks. Provide magazines so children can cut out pictures of healthy foods.

b. Help each group make a mobile for their assigned group. Use coat hangers or paper-towel tubes, string, and paper plates of different sizes. Have children glue the pictures to the paper plates. Hang the finished plates from the hangers or tubes with string. Hang mobiles from the ceiling. Be sure the breakfast, lunch, and dinner groups have at least one food from each of the four basic food groups.

2. Life-Sized Paper Images

a. Divide the class into student pairs. Give each student pair two large sheets of butcher paper. Ask one student in each pair to lie down on one of the sheets of paper. Have the partner draw an outline of the student's body. The partners then trade places.

b. Ask the children to draw in their facial features. Then have the children cut and paste on their images pictures of the esophagus, stomach, small intestine, and large intestine. Have the children cut out their paper images. Display the images around the classroom.

3. Making Skin Prints

a. Have children make a big black spot on a sheet of paper with a soft lead pencil. Ask the children to rub their index fingers over the black spot to get a good smudge on their fingers.

b. Put a piece of scotch tape on the smudged finger. Then pull off the tape carefully and press it onto a clean sheet of paper to make an image of the children's fingerprints.

c. Encourage the children to compare their fingerprints to other children's fingerprints in the classroom. Point out that each person's fingerprints are unique. No two people in the world have the same fingerprint.

d. Have children repeat the process using the bottom of their hands or their elbows. Ask children to examine their prints very carefully to see if their skin prints the same as their finger prints. Encourage students to tell how the prints differ. Use magnifying glasses, if available.

4. Smiling Crocodile

a. This is a great project for studying foods that are good for the teeth! Read appropriate book selections about good dental habits before beginning this activity. A crocodile head pattern is provided on page 64. You will also need the following materials for each child:

> two small paper plates
> one 3" x 5" piece of green construction paper
> two cotton balls
> two 1/2" dark paper circles

Directions:

1. Glue one paper circle to each cotton ball to make the eyes. Set aside.

2. Staple the two paper plates together at one end. Cut triangular-shaped teeth. Bend in the teeth.

3. Color the top of one paper plate and the bottom of the second paper plate green, except for the teeth. These two plates form the crocodile's head.

4. Trace the eyebrow pattern onto green paper and then cut the eyebrows out. Fold under the bottom to make an edge for glue.

5. Glue the eyebrows to the top of the head. Then glue on the eyes.

b. Give each child six 3" squares of white paper. Ask the children to draw three food items that are good for the teeth. Then ask the children to draw three food items that are not good for the teeth. Make one drawing per square.

c. Encourage the children to feed the crocodiles the foods that would keep the crocodile's teeth healthy. Then have the children exchange their slips of paper with other children and repeat the experience.

5. T-Shirts

a. Ask children to bring in a T-shirt for an art activity. A letter to parents explaining the project is provided on page 58. You'll also need fabric crayons and an iron.

b. Show children how to draw a black outline of the organs in our upper bodies, such as the heart or lungs. Encourage the children to draw the organs on their T-shirts first with pencil. Then, when they are satisfied with their drawings, help the children draw over their pencil drawings with a permanent black marker. Have the students color in the body parts with fabric crayons. Place a piece of wax paper and a towel over each design. Press with a hot iron. Be sure to use the iron away from the children's work area to prevent injury.

NOTES

Science Sector

The following activities help children investigate heartbeats and breathing rates. Begin a lesson by reading a nonfiction selection relating to the activity or activities you choose.

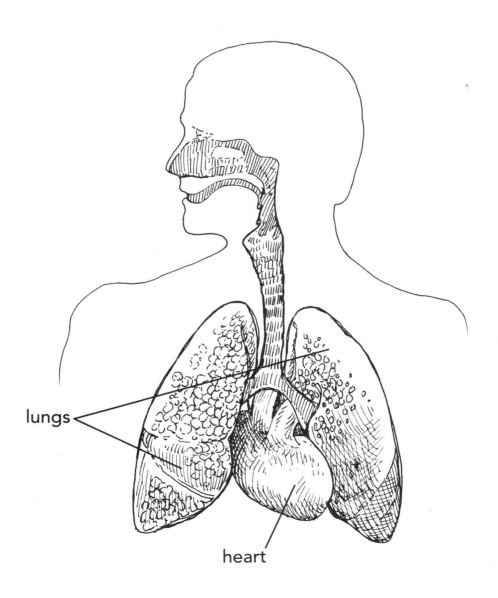

lungs

heart

1. How Hard Does the Heart Work?

a. Read a nonfiction selection about the heart to the class before beginning this activity. Some suggestions are:

   The Human Body: The Heart by Kathleen Elgin

   Your Heart and Blood by Leslie Jean LeMaster

   Bodyworks: The Kids' Guide to Food and Physical Fitness by Carol Bershad and Deborah Bernick

b. To find out how hard the heart works, have the children try to do the work of the heart with their hands. Hand out several tennis balls. Ask the children to squeeze the tennis balls very hard. Explain that the force they use to squeeze a tennis ball is similar to the force needed to pump blood through the heart.

c. Listen to the heart using a stethoscope or a short length of rubber hose and a funnel. Slip one end of the rubber hose over the small end of the funnel. The wide end of the funnel should be placed on the chest. Listen through the free end of the rubber hose. Have the children choose a partner and, in a quiet place, listen to each other's heartbeats.

2. Speeding Up Our Breathing

Ask the children to count the number of times they breathe. Time their breathing for 15 seconds. Then have the children jump up and down for 30 seconds. Immediately afterwards, have children count the number of breaths they take in 15 seconds. Compare the numbers from the two timings. Discuss why the numbers vary.

The Drama Scene

rama is a positive, fun, and fulfilling way of learning in which children can practice predicting, planning, organizing, and problem solving. Before beginning the following drama activities, read aloud an appropriate nonfiction selection.

1. Action Rhyme

Read aloud the rhyme "Can You Walk on Tiptoe?" from *Stamp Your Feet* by Sarah Hays and Toni Goffe. The second time you read the rhyme, ask the children to act out each of the movements.

2. Here Are My Hands

Read the book *Here Are My Hands* by Bill Martin, Jr., and John Archambault. Reread the book several times, encouraging the children to pantomime the actions. As a group, brainstorm other actions for each of the parts of the body named. Create new couplets using the actions the children come up with. Have children chant the rhymes while doing the actions.

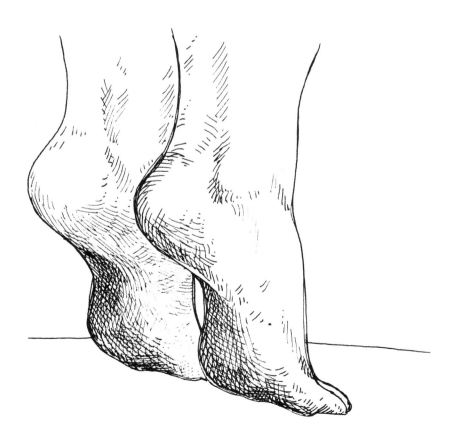

Making It Musical

Music is a wonderful way of helping children learn and remember information. Children naturally respond to rhythm and delightful lyrics. This section gives children an opportunity to learn some lyrics and songs about health.

1. Good Health

"Good Health" is a song from *Sunny Songs* by CKRB Publishing Co., P.O. Box 4023, Cerritos, California 90703-4203. Children will enjoy singing this song to the tune of "The Muffin Man." If you cannot find this song, help the children make up their own health-conscious lyrics to "The Muffin Man" melody.

2. Looby Loo

a. Introduce or review the song "Looby Loo" with your students. When the children are familiar with this song, begin changing the lyrics as a group to come up with verses having to do with health or growth.

b. Write a draft of the children's new song on chart paper. Then help the children make any revisions necessary to make their song sound just right. Arrange for the class to sing their song to another class.

Dear Parent,

For the next few weeks, our class will be studying the topic of growing up healthy. Your child will be listening to and reading books, graphing information, writing, singing songs, and exercising. To make this unit even more successful, we will need the following materials from home (if you have them). All materials will be returned at the end of the unit.

1. A baby snapshot.

2. An item of your child's baby or toddler clothing.

3. A baby toy your child played with.

4. An article of clothing from a year ago that is now too small.

5. An inexpensive T-shirt that fits (not an over-sized T-shirt, please) to be colored with fabric crayons.

Thank you for your help.

Sincerely,

Growing Up Healthy © 1992 Fearon Teacher Aids

Dear Parent,

For the next week, our class will be learning about taking good care of our teeth. Enclosed is a calendar to help your child keep a record of how often he or she brushes his or her teeth. Please help your child complete the calendar enclosed and return it to class on _____.

Thank you for your help with this activity.

Sincerely,

Name _____

Tooth Calendar for the
Week of _____

Sunday	Monday	Tuesday	Wednesday	Thursday	Friday	Saturday

EXERCISE CLUB
Membership Card

_____

is a member of the

_____

Exercise Club

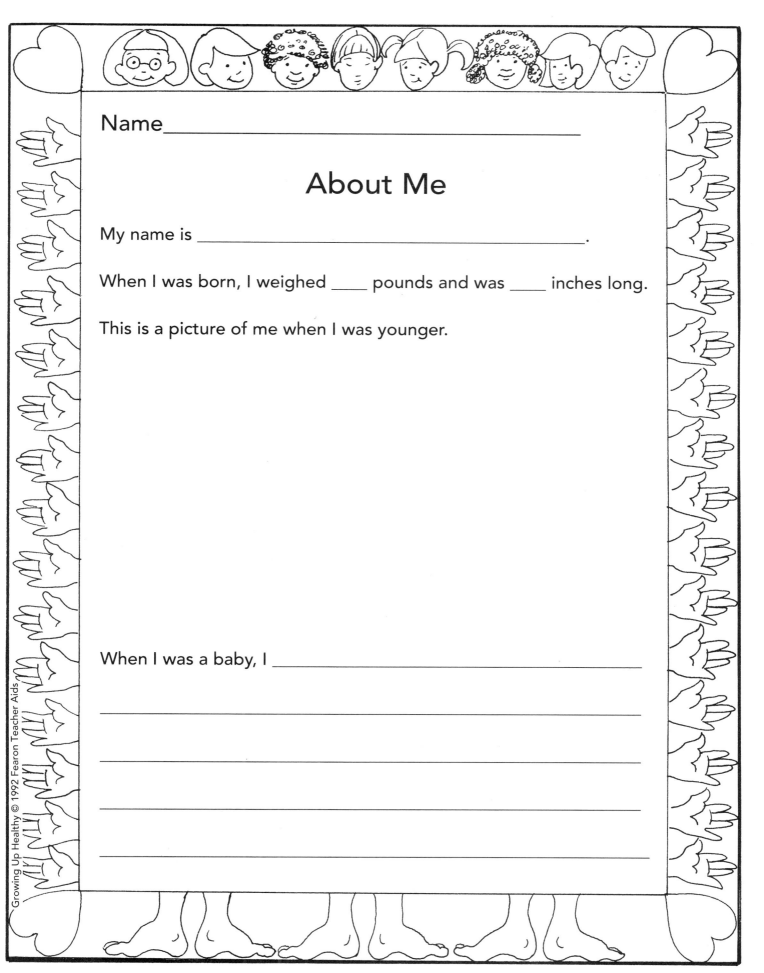

Name_____

About Me

My name is _____.

When I was born, I weighed ____ pounds and was ____ inches long.

This is a picture of me when I was younger.

When I was a baby, I _____

_____

_____

_____

_____

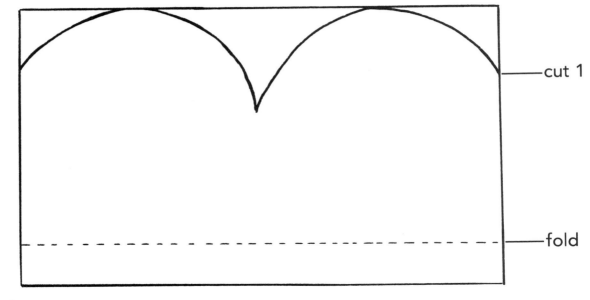

eyebrows

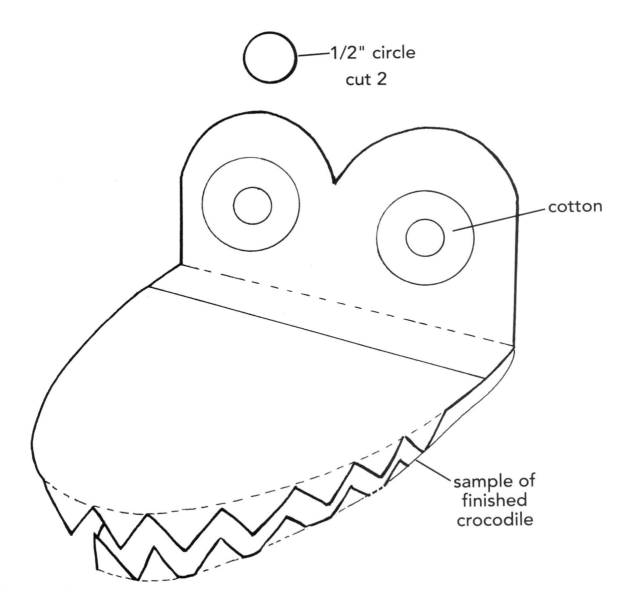

1/2" circle

cut 2

cotton

sample of
finished
crocodile